THE LATTER GLORY OF GOD REVEALED OFFICIAL WORKBOOK

HOW TO WALK UNDER THE BLESSING OF THE GLORY CLOUD

GUILLERMO MALDONADO

DESTINY IMAGE

CONTENTS

INTRODUCTION

Welcome, dear reader, to a transformative journey through "The Latter Glory of God Revealed Official Workbook." This workbook is designed not only as a companion to the teachings and revelations you've encountered in "The Latter Glory of God Revealed" but also as a practical guide to integrate these profound truths into your daily life. Here, we embark on a deep dive into the heart of God's manifest presence, exploring how His glory is not just a historical phenomenon but a living, breathing reality in the lives of believers today.

PURPOSE OF THIS WORKBOOK

The primary aim of this workbook is to equip you, the reader, with the necessary tools and understanding to become an effective carrier of God's glory. As you progress through the sections, you will engage with curated content meant to challenge, inspire, and transform your spiritual walk. Each chapter is meticulously designed to build upon the last, creating a comprehensive narrative that guides you deeper into the mysteries of God's presence.

WHAT TO EXPECT

- **Deep Biblical Insights**: The workbook revisits the pivotal moments and teachings from the book, providing deeper biblical insights into the nature of God's glory. Each passage and explanation is carefully chosen to enhance your understanding of scripture and its application to the concept of God's manifest presence in your life.
- **Practical Applications**: Beyond theoretical knowledge, this workbook offers practical steps to apply the lessons learned. Whether it's through actionable steps, reflective questions, or journaling prompts, you will find numerous opportunities to actively practice living in the reality of God's glory.
- **Personal Reflection**: Reflection is a crucial element of spiritual growth. This workbook encourages you to reflect deeply on your personal experiences with God's glory, fostering a space for honest self-assessment and spiritual renewal.
- **Community Interaction**: Recognizing the importance of fellowship in spiritual growth, some exercises and discussions are designed to be conducted within a community or small group setting. This communal approach helps reinforce the teachings and provides support as you explore these profound truths together.
- **Transformative Challenges**: Each section includes challenges that are meant to stretch your faith and

encourage a deeper engagement with God. These challenges will prompt you to step out in faith, applying what you've learned in real-world scenarios.

KEY TAKEAWAYS

- **Understanding God's Sovereignty**: Grasp the fullness of God's sovereignty as revealed through His glory. This workbook helps you understand that God's supreme authority and power are active and relevant in today's world.

- **Becoming a Carrier of Glory**: Learn what it means to not only experience God's glory but to actively carry it into every environment you enter. This transformative concept is central to the workbook, emphasizing your role as a modern-day Ark of the Covenant.

- **Miraculous Living**: The teachings in this workbook pave the way for living a life that regularly experiences and manifests the miraculous. You'll explore how to operate in faith that moves mountains and brings heaven to earth.

- **Spiritual Authority**: You'll be equipped to walk in the spiritual authority that Christ has delegated to His followers. This includes overcoming spiritual adversaries and influencing the earthly realm for God's Kingdom.

- **Prophetic Insight and Action**: Engage with exercises that enhance your sensitivity to the Holy Spirit's leading, fostering a prophetic insight that not only foretells God's plans but actively participates in bringing them to fruition.

A CALL TO ACTION

As you turn each page, consider this workbook an invitation to step into a new realm of faith and spiritual understanding. The glory of God is not a distant or unreachable concept but a tangible presence that you are meant to carry. Through your journey with this workbook, may you find yourself transformed, equipped, and fervently walking in the latter glory of God.

Prepare your heart and mind for what is more than just a study; it's an encounter with the divine that promises to change your life forever. Let's begin this journey together, with hearts open and spirits expectant, ready to receive and manifest the glory of God in ways we have never seen before.

Welcome to "The Latter Glory of God Revealed Official Workbook"—where your transformation into a bearer of His glory begins.

~

CHAPTER 1

ICHABOD, THE LOST GLORY

"Arise, shine; for your light has come! And the glory of the Lord is risen upon you." (Isaiah 60:1, NKJV).

This verse reminds us that despite past failures or spiritual slumber, the opportunity to experience and manifest God's glory is present if we turn to Him with sincere hearts.

In these times, often referred to as the "end times" in the Bible, it's crucial for us as Christians to understand the season we are living in. These times are marked by significant changes that pave the way for the second coming of Jesus. In this chapter, we explore why **End Times Awareness** is vital for preparing ourselves for these transformations, which affect both the spiritual and physical realms. Understanding this is key to aligning with God's divine plan.

At the heart of this discussion is the concept of "Ichabod," meaning the glory has departed. The story of Israel losing the Ark of the Covenant serves as a stark reminder of what happens when we stray from God's presence due to disobedience and moral decay. This biblical lesson warns us of the severe consequences of moving away from God and highlights the **Concept of Ichabod** as a central theme.

As believers, we are promised a future filled with God's overwhelming presence—a **Promise of Latter Glory** that is greater than anything we've experienced before. This isn't just comforting; it's transformative and should guide our daily lives and spiritual commitments.

However, to reach this divine presence, we must first **Restore Spiritual Vitality**. Many of us have become complacent, following religious routines instead of fostering a true relationship with the Holy Spirit. Breaking free from this spiritual slumber is crucial for experiencing the fullness of God's glory.

We also discuss how to deepen our encounters with God, explaining the **Transition from First to Latter Glory**. This isn't just about changing experiences but about a profound deepening of our relationship with God through continuous growth and renewal.

Miracles and supernatural events play a vital role in our spiritual journey. My travels and ministry work have shown me incredible miracles, especially in challenging places like Myanmar. These miracles prove the **Role of Supernatural Experiences** in showcasing God's power, even in the darkest situations.

Yet, a significant challenge in our spiritual walk is overcoming the **Dangers of Religiosity**—the bondage of empty religious practices that replace genuine faith. True spiritual vitality isn't about rituals; it's about a heartfelt connection with the Holy Spirit.

Impartation of Spiritual Gifts is crucial as well. These gifts aren't just for personal growth; they empower us to impact our communities and the world. They are activated through genuine encounters with God, enabling us to reflect His power and love.

We must also heed the lessons from the past about the

Consequences of Losing God's Glory. The story of Eli and his sons, who ignored God's commands, led to the loss of God's presence and serves as a reminder of the need for obedience and holiness.

Finally, this chapter concludes with a **Call to Holiness and Repentance.** This is a direct appeal to each of us to examine our lives, turn away from sin, and embrace holiness as the path to experiencing and retaining God's glory.

Thank you for joining me in this exploration. My prayer is that as you reflect on these truths, you will find your path to living under God's magnificent glory.

REFLECTIVE QUESTIONS:

1. What does the concept of "Ichabod" reveal about the importance of God's presence in our lives?
2. How can we identify signs of spiritual slumber in our own lives, and what steps can we take to awaken from it?
3. In what ways might religiosity be hindering our personal relationship with the Holy Spirit?
4. Reflect on a time when you experienced God's glory. What were the circumstances, and how did it transform you or others around you?
5. How can the modern church avoid the fate of Eli's priesthood and maintain the presence of God's glory?

ACTIONABLE STEPS:

- **Cultivate** a Deeper Relationship with the Holy Spirit: Begin by setting aside dedicated time each day for prayer and meditation on the Scriptures, specifically asking the Holy Spirit to reveal more of His wisdom and presence to you.
- **Equip** Yourself with Knowledge of God's Word: Commit to a systematic study of the Bible to understand the characteristics of God's glory and His expectations for holiness and obedience among His people.
- **Engage** in Spiritual Renewal Activities: Participate in church retreats, spiritual seminars, or revival meetings that focus on deepening the believers' experiences of God's presence and power.

JOURNALING PROMPT:

Reflect on your current spiritual condition. Are there areas in your life where you feel the glory of God is not as manifest as it could be? Write about these areas and what changes you can commit to making to see His glory restored in your life.

CHAPTER 2

LEADING CAUSES FOR ICHABOD IN THE CHURCH

"Create in me a clean heart, O God, and renew a steadfast spirit within me." (Psalm 51:10, NKJV).

This verse reminds us that the restoration of God's glory begins within each of us as individuals, calling for personal repentance and renewal.

In this chapter, we delve into the main reasons why many churches experience the absence of God's glory, a state known as "Ichabod." To set the stage, let me share a powerful event that took place in Lima, Peru. There, God's presence was so powerful that it led to incredible healings and the salvation of many souls. This vivid example demonstrates what can happen when **Miraculous Manifestations of God's Glory** are present.

Understanding the **Significance of God's Glory** is crucial. Without it, our churches can become spiritually dry, lacking the power and divine presence that are so clearly depicted in the

Bible. Where God's glory is present, there is vibrant life and supernatural power, essential for an impactful church.

Sin and Iniquity stand out as the primary reasons for the loss of God's glory. Tracing back to the first human disobedience in Eden, these have continued to pull humanity away from closeness with God. The fall of Adam and Eve not only introduced sin but led to a loss of divine honor and authority, illustrating the devastating impact of disobedience.

This takes us to the **Moral Corruption of the Priesthood**. The biblical account of Eli and his sons is a stark reminder of how moral failings in leadership can lead to the loss of God's presence, affecting entire communities.

Another major issue is **Compromising Principles and Truths**. When church leaders or believers prioritize personal comfort or gain over God's commands, it erodes the church's spiritual foundation and leads to the withdrawal of His glory. This kind of compromise can quietly destroy a church's spiritual vitality.

The **Loss of the Fear of God** is particularly alarming. Reverence and awe for God are foundational for maintaining His presence in our lives. Without this fear, we risk descending into moral decay, much like the society described in the days of Noah.

The chapter addresses the dire consequences for churches that have strayed from their biblical foundations and lost their reverence for God. Such churches experience a significant withdrawal of divine presence, leaving their services powerless and their rituals empty.

This chapter serves as a **Call to Repentance and Restoration**. It is a heartfelt plea for us to return to God, realign our lives and congregations with His Word, and reestablish the reverence and holiness that attract His glory.

Finally, I offer **Practical Steps for Restoration**, which guide us on how to reintroduce God's manifest presence into our churches. This involves heartfelt repentance, adherence to biblical truths, and a committed prayer life.

Thank you for joining me on this exploration. My hope is that this discussion sparks a renewed desire within you to seek God's glory anew, purify your heart, and commit to living in His holy presence.

REFLECTIVE QUESTIONS:

1. How have you personally witnessed the impact of **God's glory** in a church setting?
2. What role does personal **sin and iniquity** play in diminishing God's presence in one's life and in the church?
3. Can you identify areas in your church or spiritual community where **compromises** might be affecting the manifestation of God's glory?
4. What does the **'fear of God'** mean to you, and how can it be effectively cultivated in the church today?
5. Reflect on the current spiritual state of your church; what practical steps can be taken to **restore God's glory** if it has been lost?

ACTIONABLE STEPS:

- **Cultivate Repentance and Transparency**: Foster an environment where confession and repentance are encouraged and facilitated. This helps in clearing the path for God's glory to return.

- **Equip the Congregation with Biblical Truths**: Strengthen the church's foundation by providing sound biblical teaching that emphasizes the seriousness of sin and the necessity of holiness.
- **Engage in Consistent Prayer and Worship**: Organize regular prayer and worship sessions dedicated to seeking God's presence and asking for His glory to fill the church once again.

Journaling Prompt:

Reflect on your relationship with God. Are there areas of sin or compromise that need to be addressed to experience a fuller manifestation of God's glory? Write down your thoughts and any commitments you feel led to make.

CHAPTER 3
BRING BACK THE CHABOD OF GOD

**"Seek the LORD and His strength; Seek His face evermore!"
(1 Chronicles 16:11, NKJV).**

Let this be a daily reminder to pursue the presence of God with perseverance and passion.

As we navigate the pages of this workbook together, we arrive at a crucial chapter titled "Bring Back the Chabod of God." Here, we face the significant challenge within the Body of Christ—restoring the glory that has seemingly slipped away from us. Our mission is clear: to recapture the profound presence of God that the early Church experienced, a presence that empowered them despite severe persecution and transformed lives through miraculous events.

Reflecting on the state of our spiritual lives today, it's clear that we are missing something vital. The early Church, which we look up to as our spiritual forebearers, thrived under **God's powerful presence.** They witnessed **miraculous transformations** that seem far removed from our experience today. This loss, I believe, stems from sin—our wrongdoings and the gradual corruption that has infiltrated our leadership, pulling us away from the holy presence we desperately need.

The absence of **God's glory** has profound consequences, not only in our spiritual lives but across our communities. It manifests in rampant health issues, moral decay, and a pervasive spiritual malaise. These aren't merely social issues; they're spiritual emergencies calling for the restoration of God's transformative power.

Why does sin create such a barrier between us and God? It's because our wrongdoings build walls that hide His face from us, preventing our prayers from reaching Him. This isn't just a theological concept; it's a reality that affects our ability to feel God's presence and protection. Isaiah puts it plainly: our sins have separated us from God (Isaiah 59:2), and only through **true repentance** can we tear down these walls.

"Ichabod" signifies the absence of **God's glory**, a term we encounter in the Bible when God's presence withdrew from Israel due to their disobedience. Today, we face a similar threat. If we don't address the sins in our lives, we risk living in an Ichabod state—devoid of God's glory.

There is hope, however! **Repentance** is the key to restoring God's glory. This process requires a heartfelt turning away from sin and a genuine return to God's ways, as exemplified by King David in his fervent prayers for forgiveness and renewal (Psalm 51:9-10).

We can't walk this path of repentance alone; we need the **Holy Spirit**. He convicts us of our sins and leads us into all truth, guiding us back to righteousness. The Spirit shows us the parts of our lives needing change and gives us the strength to make those changes.

As we seek to regain the lost glory of God, there are practical steps we can undertake. It starts with quiet moments of prayer, extends to daily Scripture study, and manifests in actions within our communities. Each step is an act of obedience, a movement toward God's heart.

Imagine the transformations possible if God's glory once again filled our lives. The Bible is filled with accounts of miraculous healings and liberations—this is the power of God's tangible presence. This is the divine presence we aim to see restored in our midst.

The recovery of God's glory is deeply connected to our dedication to prayer and intercession. Through these spiritual practices, we not only seek God's face but also stand in the gap for others, pleading for divine intervention in our lives and our world.

Envision a Church imbued with God's glory—a Church where every gathering is a testimony to God's power, where every service demonstrates His transformative ability. This is the Church we are called to be, a beacon of divine light in a troubled world.

As we ponder these truths, let us recommit to seeking God's glory. Let it be our heart's cry and our daily pursuit, for in His presence is the fullness of joy, and at His right hand are pleasures forevermore.

REFLECTIVE QUESTIONS

1. How does the loss of God's glory affect our personal and community life?
2. In what ways have you seen the consequences of sin manifest in your own life or community?
3. What specific sins or behaviors might be hindering the presence of God in your life?

4. How can the Church today embody the characteristics of the early Church that walked in God's glory?

5. What role does the Holy Spirit play in your understanding and practice of repentance?

ACTIONABLE STEPS

- **Cultivate a Prayerful Heart**
- Begin each day by asking the Holy Spirit to reveal areas of sin that need repentance. Dedicate at least 15 minutes to silent prayer, reflecting on the need for God's presence.
- **Equip with the Word**
- Commit to a daily Bible study focusing on scriptures that discuss God's holiness and the importance of living a life free from sin. Share insights with a prayer partner or small group.
- **Engage in Community Restoration**
- Organize or participate in a community service project that aims to address and heal one of the societal issues highlighted in the chapter, such as addiction recovery or family counseling.

JOURNALING Prompt

Reflect on the current state of your spiritual life. Write about areas where you feel God's glory might be lacking and what steps you can take to restore His presence in those areas.

CHAPTER 4
THE RESTORATION OF THE GLORY

**"Arise, shine; for your light has come! And the glory of the
Lord is risen upon you." (Isaiah 60:1, NKJV)**

In our exploration within "The Restoration of the Glory,"
we delve into our origins, our fall, and the divine pathway
back to the presence of God, centralizing on the transformative role of Jesus Christ.

THE ORIGINAL STATE OF HUMANITY IN GLORY

We began in perfection, dwelling directly in **God's glorious
presence.** This was our natural state, where direct communion
with God was uninterrupted. Yet, through deception and sin,
introduced by Satan, humanity lost this close connection,
leaving us all in a spiritual deficit, as highlighted in Romans 3:23.
This scripture reminds us of our universal **fall from glory.**

THE CONSEQUENCE OF THE FALL

The fall significantly altered our existence, distancing us from **living in God's glory** and thrusting us into a world filled with challenges and a sense of separation from the divine. This shift was not merely spiritual but impacted our everyday experiences and perceptions of life and morality.

DIVINE PLAN FOR RESTORATION

However, the narrative takes a hopeful turn with God's master plan for our redemption, intricately woven through the promise of **restoration via Jesus Christ**. Acts 3:19-21 lays this out succinctly, pointing to repentance and renewal as our pathway back to God, emphasizing a return to our foundational state.

JESUS, THE RESTORER OF GLORY

Jesus stands at the heart of our restoration. His mission on earth was not just about teaching or performing miracles but fundamentally about bridging the vast gap created by sin. He is our direct link back to God, restoring us to the **glory from which we fell**.

THE IMPENDING END-TIME GLORY

As history marches towards its climax, the promise of God's overwhelming glory becomes increasingly apparent. Isaiah 60:1-3 assures us that even as darkness grows, **God's glory will shine ever brighter**, acting as a beacon to all nations and drawing people from every corner of the earth to His light.

GLOBAL MANIFESTATION OF GOD'S GLORY

Our missions, such as the recent trip to Pakistan, serve as concrete examples of God's glory manifesting today. Despite intense persecution, God's presence broke through dramatically, affirming that **His glory is active and transformative**, capable of reaching even the most hostile environments.

END-TIME REVIVAL AND THE FINAL HARVEST

This unfolding glory is not isolated but part of a grander divine scheme leading to a worldwide revival. This revival is set to usher in an unprecedented **harvest of souls**, signaling a monumental shift in the spiritual landscape as millions turn to God.

CHRIST'S ULTIMATE LORDSHIP

At the center of this global movement is Jesus. His death and resurrection did more than save us; they reinstated us into the realm of **God's glory**. His lordship confirms His supreme authority over all creation and His pivotal role in our personal and collective restoration.

LOOKING FORWARD TO CHRIST'S RETURN

The anticipation of Jesus' return encapsulates the culmination of God's restoration plan. This event promises to gather a restored Church, one that has been fully restored to **God's glory**, ready to meet Christ. This is not just a future event but a pivotal moment we actively prepare for through our faith and actions today.

As we engage with these profound truths, let us recommit to living lives that reflect God's glory. Let's actively participate in this incredible story of divine restoration, readying ourselves for the greater glory that awaits us.

REFLECTIVE QUESTIONS

1. How does understanding our original state in God's glory change your view of humanity's purpose?
2. What personal changes does the concept of restoration inspire in your life?
3. How can we practically prepare for the 'mega-glory' that is promised at the end of times?
4. In what ways can you participate in the global manifestation of God's glory today?
5. What does Jesus' role as the Restorer of Glory mean to you personally?

ACTIONABLE STEPS

- **Cultivate a Heart of Repentance:** Dedicate time daily to seek God in prayer, asking for a deeper revelation of His glory and for personal restoration in areas where you have fallen short.
- **Equip Yourself with Knowledge:** Study biblical prophecies and teachings about the end times and Christ's return. Educate yourself and others about the significance of these events for the Church today.
- **Engage in Proclaiming the Gospel:** Actively participate in evangelism and missions, both locally and globally, to contribute to the final harvest by

sharing the message of restoration through Jesus
Christ.

23

Journaling Prompt

Reflect on your personal journey with God. Consider the areas in your life where you need restoration. Write a prayer asking God to restore His glory in these areas, and commit to steps you can take to align more closely with His divine plan.

24

CHAPTER 5

THE EARTH WILL BE FILLED WITH HIS GLORY

Remember, God is still at work in His world and in our lives. As we embrace His promises, let us be anchored in the assurance that "the earth will be filled with the knowledge of the glory of the Lord, as the waters cover the sea."

"For the earth will be filled with the knowledge of the glory of the LORD, as the waters cover the sea." - Habakkuk 2:14 NKJV

In the chapter "The Earth Will Be Filled with His Glory," I recount the profound experiences from our mission in Chiapas, Mexico, where **God's glory** was manifest in ways that both affirmed and stretched our faith. This chapter draws from the prophecy in Habakkuk 2:14, which states, "For the earth will be filled with the knowledge of the glory of the Lord, as the waters cover the sea." This verse sets the framework for understanding the supernatural events we witnessed, connecting them directly to **God's promises**.

Our experiences in Chiapas were a powerful testimony to the

Prophetic Fulfillment of Habakkuk 2:14 being fulfilled today. It was a vivid reminder that the promises of Scripture are not just historical, but are alive and active, continually unfolding in our lives.

In Chiapas, something truly unprecedented occurred. The local mayor gave our team permission to use the city hall for our gatherings, where many locals came to accept Christ. This event marked a significant spiritual milestone for the area, illustrating the **Supernatural Encounters in Chiapas, Mexico.**

One of the most stirring miracles we witnessed was the miraculous creation of testicles for a young boy who was born without them. This moment wasn't just a physical transformation; it was a powerful **Miracle of Organ Creation**, manifesting God's care and attention to the individual needs of His people.

From the very start of our ministry there, the **presence of God** was palpable. We saw firsthand how His presence could **transform lives**—restoring people to God and mending broken relationships. This is the essence of what it means to experience God's glory.

The "latter glory" refers to a future time when **God's glory will be revealed** more profoundly than ever before. Understanding this **Concept of the Latter Glory** is key to grasping the scale and impact of what we expect to witness in the days to come.

The world is experiencing upheavals—economically, politically, and socially. Yet, in the midst of these challenges, **God's glory** is becoming more apparent. These global events are part of God's plan to set the stage for a greater **revelation of His glory**.

The chapter shares numerous testimonies of miraculous healings—people being freed from chronic illnesses and disabilities. These stories are tangible evidence of **God's glory** and are intended to bolster our faith in **God's power** today.

Historically, **God's glory** has been manifested in various forms—such as clouds, fire, and bright light. These biblical accounts help us identify the manifestations of **God's glory** and encourage us to expect His powerful presence in our times.

Isaiah 60:1-3 is a prophetic call for believers to actively participate in revealing **God's glory**. This call is not passive; it is a directive to engage actively with the divine work unfolding around us, urging us to **Arise and Shine**.

The chapter closes with a look forward to a global movement characterized by **God's glory**, which promises divine preservation, health, and abundance. This vision is not only hopeful but also a call to action for every believer, marking the **Anticipation of the End-Time Glory Movement**.

REFLECTIVE QUESTIONS

1. How do the miracles in Chiapas reflect the biblical concept of the "latter glory" and its significance for today's church?
2. In what ways have you personally experienced or witnessed the transformative power of God's presence in your life or community?
3. How can the relationship between global shaking and the increase of God's glory influence your perspective on current world events?
4. What practical steps can you take to "arise and shine" in your own context, reflecting God's glory to those around you?
5. How does the anticipation of the end-time glory movement shape your understanding of your role and responsibilities as a believer in today's world?

ACTIONABLE STEPS

- **Cultivate a Heart for Miracles**: Encourage yourself regularly by remembering and meditating on the testimonies of God's miraculous power. Let these stories build your faith and anticipation for what He can do through you.
- **Equip with Knowledge of God's Word**: Deepen your understanding of the prophecies about the latter glory. Being well-versed in these scriptures can help you recognize and be part of God's movements in today's world.
- **Engage in Prophetic Prayer**: Commit to engaging in prayer that aligns with God's prophetic promises. Pray for God to work powerfully in your life and community, just as He did in Chiapas, bringing about miraculous changes.

JOURNALING Prompt

Reflect on a time when you felt a significant presence of God in your life. How did it transform your perspective or situation? What does this encounter teach you about the nature of God's glory and its impact on your faith journey?

CHAPTER 6

THE LATTER GLORY REVEALED

Let us be encouraged that the glory of God is not just a distant reality but a present and active force in our lives. As we seek to understand and experience His glory, may our lives reflect His supernatural essence.

"But we all, with open face beholding as in a glass the glory of the Lord, are changed into the same image from glory to glory, even as by the Spirit of the Lord." - 2 Corinthians 3:18 NKJV

In the chapter titled "The Latter Glory Revealed," I share with you deep insights into experiencing God's glory. Unlike natural knowledge that we can understand through reasoning, the spiritual realm, especially God's glory, is grasped through revelation. This means one can only truly experience and walk in God's glory when it has been spiritually revealed to them.

Understanding **God's supernatural characteristics** is essential. God is infinite, eternal, and unchanging in His holiness, justice, and goodness. These are not just attributes; they are the essence of who He is. When we truly worship God, we connect deeply with these aspects of His character. I recall an event in Guatemala where our worship brought us closer to God, making His presence so tangible that spontaneous miracles happened—people were healed, and lives were profoundly changed.

It's also crucial to understand the **contrast with worldly glory**, which is transient and based on human achievements such as fame, power, or wealth. However, God's glory is eternal, stemming from our surrender to Him and overcoming life's trials with His help.

Scripture warns us about choosing the **glory of men** over God's glory. Even during Jesus' time, many who believed He was the Messiah were afraid to confess it, fearing expulsion from the synagogue. They preferred human approval over divine approval, missing out on the true essence of God's call. King David also warned against envying those who are successful in worldly terms because their achievements do not follow them beyond this life.

The **glory of God** is about His nature—His holiness, justice, goodness, and love—displayed through His supernatural acts. This glory cannot be fabricated or manipulated; it is a profound expression of God's sovereign power. It's evident when the supernatural intersects with our natural world, resulting in miraculous transformations and healings.

During another significant event in Guatemala, a woman who had suffered immensely from medical issues experienced a miraculous healing. After years of debilitating conditions and surgeries that left her bedridden, she was healed instantly during a session of worship. This event was a clear display of God's glory—His ability to do what is humanly impossible.

This chapter calls us to be part of a **glorious church**—one that reflects God's character and power, a church that radiates His light into the darkness and manifests His glory through its actions and its people. We are encouraged not only to witness God's glory but to experience and reflect it in our lives.

As we continue on this journey together, let's aim to delve deeper into understanding and embracing God's glory. Let it change us and make us bearers of His presence wherever we go. Let's be a church that not only knows about God's glory but one that actively demonstrates it, bringing hope and transformation to those around us.

REFLECTIVE QUESTIONS

1. How does the concept of revelation being necessary to understand God's glory change your approach to spiritual growth and engagement?
2. In what ways have you witnessed or experienced the transformative power of God's glory in your own life or in your community?
3. How can distinguishing between divine glory and worldly glory affect your personal values and life decisions?
4. What role does worship play in experiencing God's glory, and how can you incorporate more intentional worship into your daily life?
5. How can the church better embody and demonstrate the glory of God in a way that impacts the broader community?

ACTIONABLE STEPS

- **Cultivate a Revelation of Glory**: Spend time in prayer and meditation, asking God to reveal His glory to you in deeper ways. This can transform your understanding and experience of God's presence.
- **Equip Yourself with Scriptural Insights**: Study biblical passages that discuss God's attributes and glory. This will help you gain a clearer understanding of what God's glory really entails and how it differs from worldly concepts of glory.
- **Engage in Community Worship**: Actively participate in or facilitate worship sessions within your community that focus on experiencing God's glory. Use these opportunities to foster a deeper collective encounter with God.

JOURNALING Prompt

Reflect on a moment when you felt a profound sense of God's presence. How did this experience change your perspective on God's glory? What did it teach you about the nature of divine revelation and its impact on your faith journey?

CHAPTER 7

JESUS IS THE GLORY OF THE LORD

Let us be uplifted by the knowledge that in recognizing Jesus as the sovereign King, we see the glory of God made manifest in our lives. His rule brings not just authority, but the full manifestation of divine love and justice.

"But we all, with unveiled face, beholding as in a mirror the glory of the Lord, are being transformed into the same image from glory to glory, just as by the Spirit of the Lord." - 2 Corinthians 3:18 NKJV

In the chapter titled "Jesus Is the Glory of the Lord," I delve into how the concept of kingship directly relates to Jesus, which can be complex for those of us from democracies where kings aren't part of everyday governance. Traditionally, a king has absolute control over his territory, shaping the nation's destiny. This backdrop is crucial for understanding Jesus Christ, not just as a historical figure, but as the reigning King over all creation, across all time.

Jesus Christ, our Lord, embodies the ultimate manifestation

of God's glory in our era. Unlike earthly rulers confined by borders, Jesus's kingdom spans the entire universe, visible and invisible. His authority, confirmed by His resurrection, surpasses all, making Him the sovereign King whose reign was proclaimed when He declared to His disciples, "All authority has been given to Me in heaven and on earth."

This statement is pivotal because it underscores that no other power can match His. Jesus stands supreme as the **King of kings and Lord of lords**, His dominion everlasting and all-encompassing. This isn't just about historical or spiritual significance; it's about the ongoing reality of His rule.

Scripture is clear that all earthly rulers, no matter how powerful, must ultimately bow to Jesus. His authority extends over all creation, demanding submission from every ruler, king, and authority. Every knee will bow to Him, recognizing His ultimate power, whether through worship or forced acknowledgment of His majesty.

At the core of this chapter is the assertion that Jesus is the tangible **Glory of God.** This glory is not an abstract concept—it is personified in Jesus. When we discuss God's glory, we are really talking about Jesus Himself. He perfectly represented God's character—His grace, truth, and love—during His time on earth.

Recognizing Jesus in this light transforms our understanding of authority and governance, reshapes our approach to power, and redefines our interaction with the divine. It also changes our perception of victory and dominion, highlighting that true power and glory are demonstrated through service, sacrifice, and ultimately, resurrection, rather than through earthly triumphs.

By acknowledging Jesus as the supreme King, we gain a deeper understanding of our purpose and calling. We are invited not merely to observe His reign but to actively participate in His eternal kingdom, characterized by life, justice, and peace. As His followers, we are called to reflect His love and authority in our daily lives, relationships, and stewardship of the world.

This revelation of Jesus as the **King of Glory** calls us to a life marked by divine purpose and power, focusing not on temporary gains but on eternal significance.

REFLECTIVE QUESTIONS

1. How does the concept of Jesus as both King and the embodiment of God's glory change your understanding of His role in the universe and your life?
2. In what ways can recognizing Jesus' authority over all creation influence your daily decisions and interactions?
3. How does the eternal nature of Jesus' kingship provide comfort or challenge in your personal faith journey?
4. Reflect on a time when you experienced or witnessed a situation that reflected Jesus' sovereign power. What impact did this have on your faith or those around you?
5. Considering Jesus' role as a unifier of believers, how can you contribute to fostering unity within your community or church?

ACTIONABLE STEPS

- **Cultivate Reverence for Jesus' Sovereignty:** Regularly meditate on Scriptures that highlight Jesus' authority and kingship to deepen your reverence and understanding of His role as the supreme ruler.

- **Equip with Testimonies of His Power**: Share and listen to personal testimonies of how Jesus' lordship has positively impacted lives, strengthening your faith and encouraging others.
- **Engage in Communal Worship and Submission**: Actively participate in community worship that honors Jesus as King, promoting unity and collective submission to His will.

JOURNALING **Prompt**

Reflect on the areas of your life where acknowledging Jesus' sovereignty could bring transformation. How can you more fully submit to His rule and experience the fullness of His glory?

CHAPTER 8

CHARACTERISTICS OF THE GLORY

Remember, the glory of God is a profound expression of His presence and power. As you seek to experience and understand this glory, let your heart be encouraged by the promise that God is always near, actively working in and through His creation.

"And the Word became flesh and dwelt among us, and we beheld His glory, the glory as of the only begotten of the Father, full of grace and truth." - John 1:14 NKJV

In previous chapters, we've explored how the **glory of God** is not just an abstract concept but a person—Jesus Christ. Jesus embodies all that God is: His power, authority, and sovereignty, manifesting both in our world and within us. As we delve into this chapter, I want to share the distinct characteristics of this glory, which show how Jesus acts and moves, reflecting His values and principles.

For instance, Jesus's actions in manifesting His glory can vary —he might be watching over us, resting, or might even descend upon a person or place. We've discussed before that **glory is**

essentially the kingdom of eternity itself. Jesus, being eternal and not confined by time or space, is limitless and beyond what we can fully comprehend with reason alone.

One critical characteristic of God's glory is its creative power, which I have witnessed firsthand. In our ministry, we've seen extraordinary miracles where God's presence transformed the impossible into possible—organs were created, genetic diseases were healed, and even the weather changed. These events reinforce that in the realm of glory, what we consider supernatural becomes a part of natural existence.

Another aspect of God's glory is **rest**. God created all things with a built-in need for rest, including our bodies and the earth itself. For example, our bodies need several hours of sleep each night to function optimally, and similarly, the land requires periods of rest to maintain its fertility. This cycle of rest is embedded in creation and is a principle that extends to our spiritual lives as well.

Rest in the spiritual realm isn't about physical inactivity but finding a place in God where we feel secure and confident. It's about letting go of our fears, anxieties, and the heavy burdens that wear on our spirits. In this place of rest, we don't have to struggle or fight to see God's work; we simply trust and watch His glory manifest. This is what the scripture means when it says, **"Be still, and know that I am God"** (Psalm 46:10). Resting in God is the ultimate expression of faith, where we fully surrender to His timing and will.

Moreover, the glory of God is both a personal and a collective experience. It fills us individually but also manifests in community settings like the church. This collective aspect of glory unites us in shared spiritual experiences, strengthening our bonds with each other and with God.

Additionally, the glory of God is not meant to be hidden or kept secret; it's meant to be visible and tangible. We are called to experience and share this glory, which impacts all our senses. It's something we can see, touch, and feel, making the divine presence undeniable and powerful in our lives.

Ultimately, **accessing the glory of God requires faith**. Without faith, we cannot see or partake in this divine realm. It's faith that unlocks the miracles and wonders of God's glory, allowing us to witness His power in full measure.

As we continue to explore these characteristics, remember that the glory of God is dynamic and ever-present. It invites us to participate in the divine, to witness the miraculous, and to live in a realm where God's presence is an everyday reality.

Reflective Questions

1. How can we more actively remove the boundaries we place around God's actions in our lives?
2. What does resting in God's glory look like in practical terms in our daily routines?
3. How can the understanding of God's glory as both personal and corporate influence our interactions within the church community?
4. In what ways have you experienced or witnessed the creative power of God's glory in your own life or in the lives of others?
5. How does our faith play a role in accessing and experiencing the glory of God?

ACTIONABLE STEPS

1. **Cultivate** a deeper understanding of God's glory by studying scripture passages that describe His nature and actions.
2. **Equip** yourself and others by sharing testimonies of God's glory manifested in your life, encouraging faith and expectancy.
3. **Engage** in regular prayer and worship sessions specifically focused on inviting the glory of God into your personal and community life.

JOURNALING Prompt

Reflect on a moment in your life when you felt a strong sense of God's presence or saw a miraculous outcome. What were the circumstances, and how did it change your perception of God's glory?

CHAPTER 9

TRANSITIONING FROM THE FIRST TO THE LATTER GLORY

God is not finished with you yet. The best is yet to come, and the **latter glory** will surpass anything you have experienced before. Do not fear the changes ahead; embrace them with faith, knowing that God is leading you into a greater manifestation of His presence and power.

"The glory of this latter temple shall be greater than the former," says the Lord of hosts. "And in this place I will give peace," says the Lord of hosts.—Haggai 2:9 (NKJV)

During a 21-day fast in January 2021, the Lord entrusted me with a crucial mission: "Restore My glory and presence in My Church." Later, at the close of the School of the Spirit—an annual event designed to activate believers in the supernatural—after a period of fasting and praying, a profound experience unfolded. We stayed bowed and humbled before God for over four hours, crying out until His presence overwhelmingly descended upon us. At that moment, the Spirit of God declared to me, "The first glory of this house has ended, and the latter glory has begun." He then directed me to share this revelation with our leadership and the congregation.

Spiritual shifts only occur when they are declared. When those endowed with authority proclaim something from the spiritual realm, it solidifies into an earthly decree. Angels, heavenly hosts, and even malevolent spirits recognize a shift in seasons and must adhere to the new order. Today, I urge you to boldly proclaim, with the authority bestowed upon you by God, that the latter glory has commenced in your life.

This is the era prophesied in the scriptures where "Eye has not seen, nor ear heard, nor have entered into the heart of man the things which God has prepared for those who love Him" (1 Corinthians 2:9). We are living witnesses to these **divine manifestations**. Last year at CAP, our ministry's Apostolic and Prophetic Conference, we witnessed 331 documented miracles within just three days. These accounts were only a fraction of the total, as the supernatural activation of thousands of leaders who attended led to further miracles in their home congregations.

The **latter glory** encompasses all that God is set to unfold. The **first glory**, which pertained to all God had previously spoken, revealed, and performed through us, reached its pinnacle with the advent of Christ and the proliferation of the gospel globally. Now, we can affirmatively declare that the era of the church's first glory has concluded, giving way to the next.

I can attest to the manifestations of the first glory within King Jesus Ministry and across all affiliated ministries and churches globally. Many might attribute these happenings to human effort or claim them as their own, but in truth, God has worked through me, our leaders, disciples, and believers to enact His will—performing miracles, signs, and wonders. However, all glory, recognition, and honor are God's alone. We are merely vessels through His mighty works are done.

Let me share the fruits of my apostleship: over 12 million

souls brought to salvation, thousands of miracles documented, over 65,000 disciples trained, and countless lives transformed—from freeing young individuals from substance abuse and despair to restoring and strengthening marriages and families. Our influence has even reached global leaders, impacting presidents, prime ministers, and other significant figures with the gospel's power.

Our ministry has extended across more than seventy nations, with over 500 churches and ministries under my guidance, spreading the gospel's message and demonstrating God's supernatural power. We've established educational institutions and delivered extensive aid, all without incurring debt, purely by **God's grace** and for His glory.

A testament to the latter glory's power was vividly illustrated at our main conference when a woman, previously diagnosed with stage IV cancer and having undergone a hip amputation due to metastasis, experienced a miraculous regeneration of bone tissue after attending the event. This miracle, medically unexplainable, is a clear sign of the greater works promised in this new era of God's glory.

As we witness the cessation of the first glory, marked by natural progression and spiritual signals like global upheavals and personal trials, we are called to embrace the transition with faith. The conclusion of one glory is not the end but the preparation for a greater revelation. It is crucial to recognize and move with this transition, lest we stagnate and miss the fulfillment of God's promises for this new phase of unprecedented glory.

REFLECTIVE QUESTIONS

1. In what areas of your life or ministry have you noticed signs of stagnation, and how might this suggest that the first glory has concluded for you?
2. How can you better discern the times and align yourself with God's current movements?
3. What resistance to change have you encountered within yourself, and how can you address it to fully embrace the latter glory?
4. Consider a past difficulty or trial. How did it prepare you for a new phase in your spiritual life?
5. What are practical steps you can undertake to maintain a posture of transition, ensuring you are always ready for God's new assignments?

ACTIONABLE STEPS

- **Cultivate**: Develop a routine of spiritual discernment through regular prayer and fasting to recognize and adapt to God's timing and direction.
- **Equip**: Deepen your understanding of God's word by studying scriptures related to God's glory and promises, strengthening your spiritual foundation for upcoming transitions.
- **Engage**: Actively proclaim the new season of latter glory over your life, aligning your declarations with God's will to manifest His plans in your surroundings.

JOURNALING Prompt

Reflect on recent changes or challenges in your spiritual journey. Consider how these might indicate a transition into a new season of God's glory. Write down your thoughts, emotions, and aspirations regarding this shift, seeking God's guidance through each step.

∼

CHAPTER 10

HOW TO TRANSITION TO THE LATTER GLORY

Be encouraged that every step taken in obedience and every act of surrender brings you closer to the glory God has destined for you. Transformation is never easy, but it is always rewarding when it is in line with God's will.

"But we all, with unveiled face, beholding as in a mirror the glory of the Lord, are being transformed into the same image from glory to glory, just as by the Spirit of the Lord." - 2 Corinthians 3:18 (NKJV)

As we dive into this chapter, it's crucial to recognize that true change starts within ourselves. Personal transformation is foundational. Often, we wait for others to change—their attitudes, their minds, or even their hearts. Yet, real change begins only when we decide to **Necessity of Personal Change** transform ourselves.

Many of us hesitate at the edge of transformation because we fear the unknown. This fear can freeze us, preventing us from embracing the new chapters that God has planned for us. In discussing the **Fear of Change**, I want to encourage you to step beyond your comfort zone and trust in the transformative work God is eager to perform in your life.

Change should not be based on personal preference; rather, it should be led by God. **Divine Direction for Change** is about letting God guide our changes, specifically in areas that might be holding us back from spiritual growth and the manifestation of God's power.

Understanding the **Glory as a Realm of Rest** is also critical. This glory isn't about striving harder; it's about surrendering to God's work through us, allowing Him to move freely. This kind of rest requires us to let go of our urge to control everything and instead, allow God's sovereignty to lead our actions and decisions.

How we respond to the invitation to change varies widely. Some of us resist or ignore it, while others embrace or adapt to it. The **Responses to Change** section highlights that successful transition involves embracing and adapting to change. Managing change effectively means becoming proactive rather than victims of circumstance.

What holds us back from embracing change? Often, it's a **Fear of What Will Need to Change**. We might crave miracles and breakthroughs but fear the sacrifices they require. Overcoming this fear is a key step towards unlocking our blessings.

A significant barrier to change is a **Lack of Fear of God**—prioritizing human approval over divine approval. This misalignment can severely hinder our spiritual journey.

Sometimes, our hearts become hardened, and we close ourselves off to the transformative work of the Spirit. **Hardness of Heart** can lead to spiritual stagnation and even death, preventing us from fully experiencing God's transformative power.

Repentance as a Starting Point is crucial. It's the act of turning away from sin and everything that distances us from God, and it's the first step toward genuine transformation that refreshes and revives our spirit.

We often form unhealthy attachments to people, places, and things that can keep us tied to our old lives. **Breaking Unhealthy Soul Ties** involves a conscious decision to cut these ties and free ourselves for a closer walk with God.

Obedience to Divine Instructions plays a critical role in our spiritual journey. It can accelerate our progress and lead us into deeper levels of glory, or it can hinder our path if we choose disobedience. Obedience aligns us with God's timing and purposes, opening doors to blessings we might otherwise miss.

Lastly, **Spiritual Cleansing and Renewal** is essential for anyone seeking to enter into a deeper level of spiritual experience. This cleansing process is not instantaneous but a progressive journey towards purity and holiness, preparing us to carry the glory of God.

In closing, remember that each step of obedience and every act of surrender draws you nearer to the glory destined for you. Transformation might be challenging, but it's incredibly rewarding when aligned with God's will. Stay encouraged and steadfast in your journey to the latter glory.

May you find peace and strength as you walk this path of transformation, and may you see the glory of God manifest in your life as you make these changes.

REFLECTIVE QUESTIONS

1. What personal fears do you need to overcome to embrace the changes God is calling you to make?
2. How can you start to align more closely with God's

will, even when it contradicts your desires or understanding?

3. What unhealthy soul ties might be holding you back from moving forward in your spiritual journey?

4. Can you identify any areas of disobedience in your life that might be delaying your spiritual progress?

5. In what ways can you actively engage in spiritual cleansing to prepare for a higher level of glory?

ACTIONABLE STEPS

- **Cultivate a Heart of Repentance**: Regularly assess your life and repent for areas where you fall short, focusing on turning away from sin and towards God.
- **Equip Yourself with Knowledge of God's Word**: Dive deeper into scripture to understand God's will and align your actions with biblical principles.
- **Engage in Community and Accountability**: Surround yourself with a community that encourages spiritual growth and holds you accountable to your commitment to change.

JOURNALING Prompt

Reflect on the current changes God might be asking you to make in your life. How do you feel about these changes? What steps can you take today to align your life more closely with God's will?

CHAPTER 11
WALKING UNDER THE GLORY CLOUD

Remember, walking under the Glory Cloud is a privilege that brings profound blessings and protection. Embrace it fully, trusting in God's sovereignty and timing, and watch as He transforms your life and surroundings.

"But we all, with unveiled face, beholding as in a mirror the glory of the Lord, are being transformed into the same image from glory to glory, just as by the Spirit of the Lord." - 2 Corinthians 3:18 (NKJV)

I want to share with you a powerful experience. Some time ago, I was given a prophecy about leading a ministry called the Glory Cloud Ministry. Today, I see this prophecy coming true both locally and globally. The **Divine Guidance through the Glory Cloud** guides me, performing miracles and transforming every place it touches.

This **Fulfillment of Prophecy** is a true testament to God's faithfulness. He announced this through His prophet and has made it a reality in amazing ways, just as He promised. It shows how powerful and true God's promises are.

The impact of walking under this Glory Cloud is profound. It transforms everything around, turning what was once spiritual emptiness into thriving areas full of spiritual life. This **Impact of the Glory Cloud** is similar to how God led the Israelites with a cloud during their escape from Egypt.

Reflecting on **Historical Biblical Context**, I draw parallels between the journey of Israel and our experiences today under the Glory Cloud. It reminds us of God's unchanging presence and guidance.

Discussing the **Sovereignty and Power of God**, I emphasize that God's actions are not constrained by our human conditions or our level of faith. He is sovereign and does things according to His will, which we should respect and not underestimate.

One crucial lesson I share is about the **Human Limitations and God's Unlimited Power**. Despite seeing countless miracles, the Israelites limited God with their narrow mindset and lack of faith. We must learn from this and avoid the same mistakes.

The **Prophetic and Practical Implications** of the Glory Cloud are significant. It's not just a symbol; it's a powerful manifestation that heals, delivers, and protects. It shows God's kingdom at work on earth.

We also talk about the importance of learning from **Lessons from Past Mistakes**. The failures of the Israelites serve as warnings for us. They witnessed God's miracles but often responded with doubt and rebellion, leading to severe consequences.

This chapter also explores the balance between **God's Will and Human Agency**. We have the freedom to either enable or restrict what God can do in our lives based on our faith and obedience.

Lastly, I promise you the **Promises of Divine Blessings** for those who faithfully walk under the Glory Cloud. These include divine health, protection, and provision, guaranteed to those who align with God's commands.

In conclusion, walking under the Glory Cloud is an extraordinary and blessed journey. It requires faith, obedience, and an open heart to God's will. As we follow this divine guidance, we see transformations not just in our lives but also in the world around us.

I hope this inspires you to seek and recognize the movement of the Glory Cloud in your life and embrace the immense blessings it brings.

REFLECTIVE QUESTIONS

1. How have you experienced or how do you anticipate experiencing the guidance of the Glory Cloud in your life?
2. In what ways might you be limiting God's power in your life through unbelief or small-mindedness?
3. What changes can you make to better align with God's sovereign guidance as demonstrated through the Glory Cloud?
4. How does the concept of divine blessings associated with the Glory Cloud influence your faith and daily living?
5. What steps can you take to ensure you are not left behind when the Glory Cloud moves?

ACTIONABLE STEPS

- **Cultivate Awareness of God's Presence**: Actively seek to recognize and acknowledge God's presence in your daily life, fostering a deeper awareness of His guidance through the Glory Cloud.
- **Equip Yourself with Scriptural Knowledge**: Delve into biblical teachings about God's sovereignty and guidance, using scripture to understand how God has historically led His people and how He continues to lead today.
- **Engage in Faithful Obedience**: Commit to living in obedience to God's word, making conscious decisions that align with His will, ensuring you remain under the protection and guidance of the Glory Cloud.

JOURNALING Prompt

Reflect on your current spiritual journey under the Glory Cloud. Consider the ways in which you might be resisting or embracing God's guidance. What steps can you take to deepen your commitment to following where the Glory Cloud leads?

~

CHAPTER 12

CARRIERS OF THE GLORY OF GOD

As we conclude our journey through this book, I am deeply moved to challenge you to embrace your calling as a carrier of God's glory. The transformation you've undergone through these revelations is not just for your personal edification but to impact the world around you. We are designed to be vessels of His divine presence, radiating His glory wherever we go. Let me share a powerful testimony that embodies this truth.

"But we have this treasure in earthen vessels, that the excellence of the power may be of God and not of us." - 2 Corinthians 4:7 (NKJV)

Imagine being so filled with God's glory that wherever you go, you become a catalyst for miraculous transformations. This is not just a dream—it's your divine calling. Through these pages, you've learned that to carry God's glory is an extraordinary responsibility and honor.

The story of my spiritual son in Ghana vividly illustrates what it means to be a **dynamic carrier of God's glory**. Kwadwo

Bempah, after being transformed by the teachings of faith and the supernatural, witnessed a dead child return to life—an astounding miracle that drew many to Christ. His ministry exponentially grew from these divine encounters, showing us the **impact of walking in God's anointing**.

This testimony isn't just inspiring—it's a direct challenge to each of us. The **ripple effect of carrying God's glory** can lead to exponential growth in the Kingdom, as seen in Kwadwo's ministry. From small beginnings, his obedience to the call led to a thriving church with significant influence.

In the Bible, the glory of God was once contained in the Ark of the Covenant, a holy vessel that demanded respect and obedience to divine order. **Respecting God's order is crucial** for carrying His glory today. We see this through the life of King David and the tragic lesson learned when Uzzah touched the Ark. This teaches us that **divine protocols must not be ignored**.

Today, unlike the Levites who carried the Ark on their shoulders, every believer has the potential to be a carrier of God's glory. **You are a modern-day Ark of the Covenant**, with the presence of God residing in your heart through the Holy Spirit. This incredible truth should transform how we live and move in the world.

As carriers of God's glory, our lives should manifest His presence through **signs, wonders, and acts of faith**. Each act of obedience, each step taken in faith, extends the Kingdom of God on Earth. This is not just a privilege; it's a **mandate for every believer**.

Therefore, let us move forward with a clear understanding and commitment. We are called to **bear His glory not by our might, nor by our power, but by the Spirit of the Lord**. This realization should drive every decision, every action, and every word we speak.

In closing, I invite you to step into your calling with boldness and faith. Let the **light of God's glory shine through you,** transforming every darkness into light and bringing hope and life wherever you go.

REFLECTIVE QUESTIONS

1. **What personal transformations have you experienced** that indicate you are carrying God's glory?
2. **How can you increase your sensitivity** to God's presence to become a more effective carrier of His glory?
3. **What fears or hesitations might you need to overcome** to step fully into this calling?
4. **How can you practically demonstrate God's glory** in your everyday interactions and decisions?
5. **What steps will you take to ensure that God's glory is not just a concept but a reality** in your life?

ACTIONABLE STEPS

- **Cultivate a Deep Relationship with God**: Spend time daily in prayer and worship, seeking to deepen your understanding of His presence and glory.
- **Equip Yourself with Knowledge of God's Word**: Study scriptures that explain the nature of God's glory and how it operated through believers throughout the Bible.
- **Engage in Acts of Faith**: Look for opportunities to exercise your faith in real-world situations where

God's glory can manifest through healing, prophetic words, or miraculous provision.

72

JOURNALING Prompt

Reflect on your journey through this book and the transformations you've noticed in your understanding and experiences of God's glory. What are the key changes in your perception of being a carrier of God's glory, and how do you plan to implement this understanding in your daily life?

DESTINY IMAGE

Destiny Image is a prophetic Christian publisher dedicated to empowering believers through Spirit-led messages. Our mission is to equip and inspire individuals to fulfill their God-given destinies by providing transformative resources that resonate with the Charismatic and Pentecostal faith.

We specialize in books, blogs, and back cover copies that reflect prophetic insights, dynamic teachings, and testimonies of faith. Our commitment to fostering spiritual growth and kingdom impact makes Destiny Image a beacon for those seeking to deepen their relationship with God and embrace their calling in the power of the Holy Spirit.